RAF
Skellingthorpe

LANCASTER STATION AT WAR
1941 - 1945

Best Wishes

Derek Brammer

By
Derek Brammer

This Book is dedicated to my dear wife Marjorie who has shared my life for the past fifty years

Every effort has been made by the author to trace owners of any material used

First Published in Great Britain in 2010 by Tucann Books
Text © Derek Brammer All rights reserved
Design © TUCANN*design&print*

ISBN **978-1-907516-04-7**

Produced by: TUCANN*design&print*, 19 High Street,
Heighington Lincoln LN4 1RG
Tel & Fax: 01522 790009
www.tucann.co.uk

PREFACE

During the Second World War I was a young schoolboy and lived near Boultham Park in Lincoln which was only two miles away from the main gate of RAF Skellingthorpe.

This primitive wartime airfield was the closest to my home, so it is understandable that I should become interested in the airfield and activities of the two premier Lancaster squadrons of No.5 Group that flew hazardous bombing operations in the hostile skies of mainland Europe.

In 1997 after two years research I published my first book called:

"Thundering Through The Clear Air"
No. 61 (Lincoln Imp) Squadron at War".

The book was well received by the Squadron veterans, so after adding more chapters I published a 2nd Edition in 2005. ISBN 1 873257 57 0
My initial research produced far more information and photographs than I could use in that book so I decided to write about the wartime activities at RAF Skellingthorpe and the two resident squadrons, No. 50 & No. 61 Squadron.

Over the past year I have carried out more research and collected additional data and photographs in order to make this book as informative as possible.

My aim is to give the reader an insight of what life was like on a front line operational bomber station of No.5 Group Bomber Command during the Second World War.

Derek Brammer
January 2010

INTRODUCTION

On Sunday morning the 2nd June 1996 members of No.50 and No.61 Squadron Association returned once again to attend the annual Service of Remembrance at the Squadrons Memorial in Birchwood Avenue, Lincoln.

In the afternoon the Skellingthorpe Parish Council granted both Squadrons the **"Freedom of the Parish"**. This being the Highest Honour a Civic Body can bestow on a person or organisation. Afterwards approximately 100 veterans with medals proudly displayed marched behind a military band from the village Church to the Memorial garden near the Community Centre.

Later I began to wonder if the people living on the Birchwood Estate realise that their small plot of land played an important role in the defeat of Nazi Germany by being part of an RAF Bomber Command Airfield.

From 1941 to 1945 the RAF personnel at Skellingthorpe airfield were a mixed bunch consisting of British, Canadian, Australian, New Zealanders and 'Free' European nationals.

Some of the Lancaster skippers were only just twenty years of age and yet they were deemed old enough to fly a powerful highly technical machine with a gross weight of 60,000lb. They also carried the extra burden of being responsible for the safety of their six man crew.

When Ops were on and dusk approached various types of vehicles could be seen travelling to distant dispersals to drop-off the air crews near their Lancaster aircraft. After checking with their hard working ground crew that everything was in order they would chat amongst themselves or nervously smoked a last minute "Willie-Woodbine". As take off time approached cigarettes were stubbed out and the air crew would pick up their parachutes and climb aboard through the rear starboard doorway and quickly disappear inside as they took up their various crew positions. The pilot would slide back the port side cockpit window and informed the ground crew that he was ready to start engines. Once all four engines were performing correctly, chocks were waved away followed by a hiss of escaping air as the brakes were released. The aircraft then moved slowly out of the dispersal to join other aircraft winding their way in single file around the perimeter track towards the main runway. When his turn came for take-off each pilot turned his aircraft onto the runway and applied the brakes before throttling down again to a tick-over and await a green light from the Flying Control caravan. The green light from the Aldis lamp was greeted with a loud cheer from a group of off duty personnel that had congregated nearby to wish all the crews good luck and a safe return.

With engines revved and brakes released the aircraft slowly rolled forward and then quickly gained speed in a series of gentle bounces under the weight of the heavy fuel and bomb load. With a quarter of the runway remaining the aircraft slowly rose into the air and with undercarriage retracted, quickly disappeared into the failing light on the first leg of it's nocturnal operation.

Those of us who lived close by the airfield during the war years will never forget the cough and splutter of Merlin engines being started at the dispersals. Followed by the sound of 30 Lancasters taxiing around the perimeter track towards the main runway and then the din created by four Merlin engines as they powered a fully loaded Lancaster into the air. This thunderous sound was then replaced by a long laboured drone as each aircraft climbed away to join the distant Bomber Stream.

After the last aircraft had clawed it's way into the air and departed with the sound of it's laboured engines fading away, the airfield fell strangely silent.

Rural tranquillity descended once again on the surrounding woods and fields and as the group of off duty WAAFs and airmen strolled back to their billets, rabbits came out of hiding and scurried across the main runway before disappearing once again into the long grass that edged this great expanse of concrete. While in the distance ground crews could be seen tidying the dispersals in readiness for their aircraft's return. Several hours later most of them would return to this primitive airfield code named "Black Swan".

Today the old trees that once lined the narrow road to the airfields technical site, now leads to the No.50 & No.61 Squadron memorial. Marshal of the Royal Air Force Sir Arthur Harris wrote the following about the men he sent into the nightly hell of Bomber operations:

"There are no words with which I can do justice to the air crew who fought under my command. There is no parallel in warfare to such courage and determination in the face of danger over so prolonged a period ... Such devotion must never be forgotten"

CONTENTS

RAF Skellingthorpe

RAF SKELLINGTHORPE
AIRFIELD LOCATION PLAN 1941

During the Second World War the Royal Air force had 13 airfields within a 12 miles radius of Lincoln Cathedral.

One of the most unusual sites to be chosen was just outside the City boundary in a very wooded area with gravel pits near Lord Liverpool's Hartsholme Hall estate.

The site was an area of pasture known locally as Black Moor and surrounded by plantations of Birch trees.

Two miles away to the north-west along the B1378 was the small village of Skellingthorpe situated near several large woods.

This new airfield had been planned to serve as a satellite landing ground for RAF Swinderby from where No.50 and No.455 RAAF squadron flew bombing operations with their twin engine Hampdens.

Construction of the airfield started in the spring of 1941 with hutted accommodation secreted in the woods around hard strip runways.

In October of 1941 even though there was a lack of personnel accommodation, No.50 and No.455 squadron moved their Hampdens over to the newly commissioned RAF Skellingthorpe in order to allow concrete runways to be laid at RAF Swinderby.

Some of the personnel remained billeted at Swinderby until the Australian Squadron moved to RAF Wigsley in February 1942.

In June 1942 No.50 Squadron returned to Swinderby while three concrete runways were laid at Skellingthorpe.

The airfield layout at Skellingthorpe was in the adopted wartime standard consisting of three runways. The main runway was extended from the planned 1,650 to 2,000 yards in preparation for the new four engine Lancaster bomber. With the two subsidiaries each measuring 1,400 yards in length. Aircraft service areas were provided by 36 Frying Pan type hardstands scattered around the perimeter track.

The station was developed in two main areas. To the north, off Skellingthorpe Road was the main gate and technical site. This had a T2 type hangar, workshops, stores and other squadron hutted facilities. Also two communal sites, two WAAF and five male domestic sites plus sick quarters.

On the east side was a sub-technical site with a second T2 hangar and to the south a B1 type hangar, also a motor transport parking and service area.

To the south off Doddington Road, the administration site, one communal site, two male domestic sites and sick quarters. The bomb store lay to the north-west of the runways in woodland

The main runway started from Doddington Road and ran in a north-easterly direction towards Lincoln Cathedral.

The airfield facilities were to eventually accommodate two complete bomber squadrons consisting of 40 aircraft and 1,800 male and 300 WAAF personnel

Unlike the pre-war RAF Stations that had brick built barrack blocks with centrally heated dormitories. The wartime airfields only offered basic accommodation.

At RAF Skellingthorpe the domestic sites were either long wooden huts or corrugated iron Nissen huts. Each domestic site shared latrine and ablution facilities.

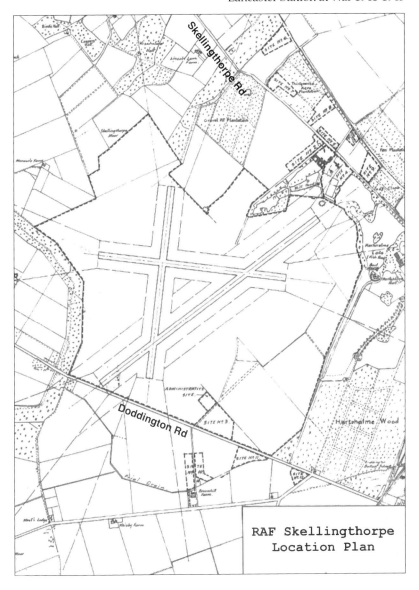

RAF Skellingthorpe
Location Plan

The number of personnel in each hut varied according to rank. When No. 61 squadron arrived at Skellingthorpe there was an accommodation shortage therefore the number of personnel in each hut was higher than the planned standard.

Some airman huts had twenty beds with little storage space. While in the same size hut, NCOs had fourteen beds and junior officers eight. Senior officers had partitioned two bed or single room accommodation with toilets and ablution facilities within the hut. Everyone was issued with three straw palliasses, two sheets, a pillow case and four blankets.

RAF Skellingthorpe Nissen hut accommodation On cold wet winter nights keeping warm and drying clothes was difficult with only one small coke stove in each hut

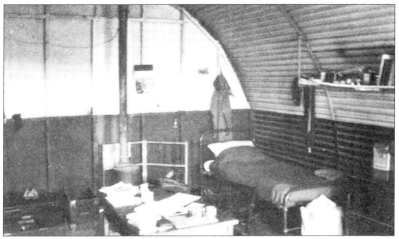

A junior Officers bed space in prime position near the heating stove

Typical Communal Site

The large Recreation Hut on the communal sites offered some comfort

RAF Skellingthorpe Airfield (Black Swan)

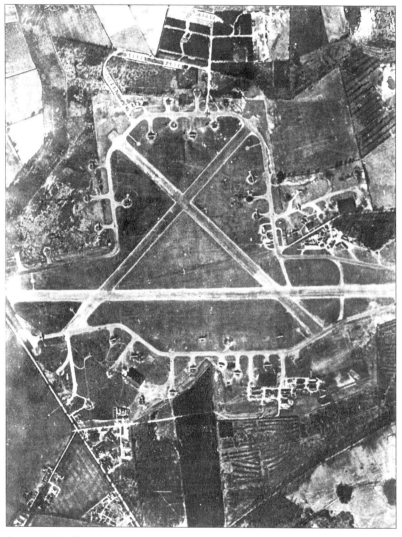

August 1944 with 29 Lancaster aircraft dispersed across the airfield. No.50 Squadron technical site and squadron support sections were above the main runway and No.61 Squadron below

No. 50 SQUADRON

Commanding Officers	Date
W/Cdr L Young	07/38
W/Cdr R T Taffe	04/40
W/Cdr N D Crockart	06/40
W/Cdr G W Gollegde	06/40
W/Cdr G Walker	12/40
W/Cdr R J Oxley	10/41
W/Cdr WM Russell	10/42
W/Cdr R McFarlane	08/43
W/Cdr F Pullen	12/43
W/Cdr A W Heward	01/44
W/Cdr R T Frogley	06/44
W/Cdr J Flint	03/45

No.50 Squadron in front of a Handley Page Hampden aircraft in 1941

No. 50 Squadron C/O Wing Commander Gus Walker (2nd right) and crew

Armourers fusing bombs before loading them aboard the aircraft

No.50 Squadron aircrew boarding their Hampden aircraft

Since the start of the war in September 1939 No. 50 Squadron flew 266 Bombing, 88 Mine laying and 14 Leaflet raids with their Hampden aircraft. They lost 57 aircraft (2.5 %) of the 2,299 sorties flown

Daybreak return from an operation

New A.V.Roe aircraft for No. 5 Group:

In April 1942 the Squadron converted to the new twin engine Avro Manchester aircraft which was larger, faster and better armed than the Handley Page Hampden. So it was welcomed as a positive development by the air crews of No.5 Group.

Unfortunately the aircrafts new Rolls-Royce Vulture engine was unreliable and resulted in many crashes and loss of experience air crew. As a result only 15 Bombing, 10 Mine laying and 9 Leaflet raids were flown in No. 50 Squadron Manchester's with an operational loss of 7 aircraft. (5.6%) of the 126 sorties flown.

A.V. Roe Manchester Mk1 R5784 at Skellingthorpe in May 1942.
Crew from L-R: Sgt. S.A. Grawler (A G)A.C. Rodger; Sgt. Wellford (W/op)
Sgt. G. Murtough (AG) P/O T.B. Cole DFC (P) P/O P.W. Rowling (N)

Manchester Mk1

V.C. HERO OF No. 50 SQUADRON

F/O Leslie Manser V C   *Victoria Cross*

Twenty year old Flying Officer Leslie Thomas Manser of No.50 Squadron took off from RAF Skellingthorpe on 30th May 1942 for Cologne on Bomber Command's first 1,000 aircraft bombing raid.

For his courageous actions during the raid was posthumously awarded the country's highest military decoration for valour, the "**Victoria Cross.**"

Extract from the London Gazette of Friday 23rd October 1942

"The KING has been graciously pleased to confer the VICTORIA CROSS on the under mentioned officer in recognition of most conspicuous bravery :-

Flying Officer Leslie Thomas Manser 66542 Royal Air Force Volunteer Reserve (Deceased) No. 50 Squadron.

Flying Officer Manser was captain and first pilot of a Manchester aircraft which took part in the mass raid on Cologne on the night of May 30th, 1942.

As the aircraft was approaching its objective it was caught by searchlights and subjected to intense and accurate anti-aircraft fire. Flying Officer Manser held on his dangerous course and bombed the target successfully from a height of 7,000 feet.

Then he set course for base. The Manchester had been damaged and was still under heavy fire. Flying Officer Manser took violent evasive action, turning and descending to under 1,000 feet. It was of no avail. The searchlights and flak followed him until the outskirts of the city were passed. The aircraft was hit repeatedly and the rear gunner was wounded. The front cabin filled with smoke; the port engine was over-heating badly.

Pilot and crew could all have escaped safely by parachute. Nevertheless, Flying Officer Manser, disregarding the obvious hazards, persisted in his attempt to save aircraft and crew from falling into enemy hands. He took the aircraft up to 2,000 feet. Then the port engine burst into flames. It was ten minutes before the fire was mastered, but then the engine went out of action for good, part of one wing was burnt, and the air-speed of the aircraft became dangerously low. Despite all the efforts of pilot and crew, the Manchester began to lose height. At this critical moment, Flying Officer Manser once more disdained the alternative of parachuting to safety with his crew. Instead, with grim determination, he set a new course for the nearest base, accepting for himself the prospect of almost certain death in a firm resolve to carry on to the end.

Soon, the aircraft became extremely difficult to handle and, when a crash was inevitable, Flying Officer Manser ordered the crew to bale out. A sergeant handed him a parachute but he waved it away, telling the non-commissioned officer to jump at once as he could only hold the aircraft steady for a few seconds more. While the crew were descending to safety they saw the aircraft, still carrying their gallant captain, plunge to earth and burst into flames.

In pressing home his attack in the face of strong opposition, in striving, against heavy odds, to bring back his aircraft and crew and, finally, when in extreme peril, thinking only of the safety of his comrades, Flying Officer Manser displayed determination and valour of the highest order".

The Lancaster Era: 1942-1945

The Manchester was a disappointment and dubbed the "Flying Coffin" by some air crew.

However unbeknown to the crews the manufacturer A. V. Roe was already flight testing a four engine replacement to be called, "Lancaster"

The existence of the Lancaster was made public on the 17th April 1942 when No.44 & No.97 Squadron made a daring daylight attack on the MAN diesel factory at Augsburg. For his heroic actions S/L John Nettleton of No.44 Squadron was awarded the Victoria Cross

In October 1942 No.50 Squadron returned to RAF Skellingthorpe after re-equipping with the new Avro Lancaster during the summer months at RAF Swinderby

No.50 Squadron Lancasters at RAF Swinderby in August 1942

No.50 Squadron carrying out training flights over Lincolnshire

No.50 Squadron Lancaster R5689 "VN-N " flown by S/L Hughie Everitt

The end of the most photographed Lancaster during 1942. On the 19th September 1942 VN-N lost power and crashed at Thurlby while returning to RAF Swinderby after a Gardening operation. (Laying sea mines)

No. 50 Squadron Lancasters set out for a bombing operation

Bombing Raids during 1942 - 1943

On the 17th October 1942 the Squadron flew on a low level daylight raid against the Schneider works at Le Creusot near the German/Swiss border which manufactured heavy guns, railway engines, tanks and armoured cars

The attacking Lancasters flying at low level over the French countryside

It was an all 5 Group operation consisting of 94 Lancasters from nine squadrons led by Wing Commander L.C. Slee of 49 Squadron. Eighty-eight aircraft attacked the factory and the other six were briefed to destroy the Montchanin power transformer station which supplied electrical power to the factory.

The only casualty was Lancaster W4774 of No.61 Squadron flown by Squadron Leader W. D. Corr DFC. Who made his attack on the transformer station at such a low level that exploding bombs caused his aircraft to crash in the target area.

During the winter months production of four engine bomber aircraft increased and Bomber Command were able to expand the number of front line bomber squadrons.

On the 5th of March 1943 Bomber Command start a four month campaign against the industrial Ruhr valley. Nicknamed "Happy Valley" by air crew. The "Battle of the Ruhr" was successful mainly due to high flying twin engine Mosquitoe Pathfinder aircraft. Who marked the targets with great accuracy using the new Oboe long range blind bombing system.

However the Happy Valley area was defended by large numbers of night fighters and a ring of heavy flak installations. By the end of July 1943 Bomber Command had lost 870 heavy bomber aircraft from front line squadrons and 6,000 highly trained air crew.

The "Battle of Hamburg" code named "Gomorrah" soon followed and is regarded as the most concentrated and successful series of raids carried out by Bomber Command during the war. This accuracy was achieve by the introduction of a new short range Air to Ground blind bombing equipment called H2S. This equipment showed the Pathfinder aircraft navigators an outline picture of the ground below their aircraft.

Also millions of silver paper strips called "Window" were dropped by the raiders as they approached the target area in order to confuse German radar.

In mid August the squadrons of No.5 and 6 Group were briefed to bomb the secrete V1 and V2 rocket research establishment at Peenemunde on the Baltic coast.

The raid was to be carried out at low level and in moonlight in order to achieve bombing accuracy and totally destroy the facility. At the briefings the crews were told that if the raid wasn't successful they would have to return the following night to complete the job.

The Bombing Master for the raid was, Group Captain John Searby. He circled the target area and controlled the attack by instructing the main force Bomb Aimers over their aircrafts VHF radio sets which Target Indicators to aim at.

Despite a successful diversionary raid on Berlin by 8 Mosquitoes. Forty aircraft (6.7%) of the main force failed to return due to intense night fighter activity as the bombers flew back over the Baltic Sea towards Denmark.

OPS ARE ON TONIGHT

Station Commander Group Captain JN Jefferson with Squadron Commanders

Early in the day the Station's Commanding Officer would be waiting in the Operations Room for a tele-printer message from Group Headquarters containing orders for the next bombing operation to be carried out by the squadrons on his bomber station. With him would probably have been the squadron Wing Commander and Intelligence Officer.

Aircrew checked the notice boards in their Mess or Squadron office to see if their name was on the Battle Order for that night. Orderlies would also awaken aircrew asleep in their billets if they have been called upon to do consecutive night operations. Weather forecasts had to be prepared by the Meteorological Officer and the Signals and Medical Officers were also notified of the impending operation.

Out on the Flight Lines:
Upon receipt of the Operation Orders the airfield became a hive of activity as the various ground staff trades set about their tasks to bring the Squadron aircraft to a state of readiness for the night's operation. Scores of airmen and WAAFs took a hand in getting every aircraft on the Squadron ready for the appointed take-off time.

Lancaster ME596 QR-H with No.61 Squadron Service Flight. The aircraft was lost on the Russelsheim raid 12/13th August 1944 with P/O G. Taylor and crew.

Operational aircraft stood up to severe punishment during the course of a bombing operation. Not only from normal wear and tear, but all too often aircraft returned with flak or night fighter cannon shell damage. Consequently its serviceability depended upon the work carried out by the Squadron ground staff. Each bomber aircraft had its own ground crew made up of men who were skilled in a particular job and headed by a corporal. He usually possessed the trade qualifications of Fitter One the highest grade of any trade in the Royal Air Force. Under his supervision were a crew of eight Aircraft hands (ACH) consisting of two Flight Mechanics (engines) and two Flight Mechanics (airframe) plus a Wireless Mechanic, Electrician, Instrument Repairer and Fitter Armourer.

During the winter months of 1943-44 both squadrons had approximately twenty Lancasters on strength and these aircraft were divided and maintained by two ground crew flights. Exercising general supervision over the ground crew on each flight was a

Sergeant of each trade, who in turn was directly responsible to a Flight Sergeant who acted as technical adviser when difficulties arose. When the ground crews reported at the Squadron hangar each morning, they were detailed to their duties, which generally meant a complete daily inspection of each aircraft.

Engine Fitters at work on QR-G

After each operation the engine mechanics were fully employed in checking fuel pipe lines for security, inspecting magnetos, looking for leaks in the fuel, oil and coolant tanks and associated components. In addition the variable pitch airscrew had to be examined and tested for its full range of movement. This task was done while the engine was running. Oil pressures and temperatures of oil and coolant were all checked together with the revolutions of the engines per minute. These, with the examination of the boost pressure, were only a few of the items that had to be noted before final clearance was given.

During this time the airframe mechanics were checking the freedom of movement of the controls and taking up slack if required. The hydraulic system of the undercarriage was looked into, tyre pressures and oil levels in air compressors were checked and the fabric and metal surfaces were carefully searched. These surfaces were closely scrutinised for damage and corrosion and then the entire aircraft was cleaned of all oil and dirt.

Meanwhile, the wireless mechanic tested the receiving and transmitting sets, accumulators were recharged, or coils replaced as necessary. The aerial wiring was followed through, and the system tested with a ground station. The aircraft's TR1154 & 55 wireless sets were of great importance to the aircrew as the equipment had to be capable of receiving and sending vital signals that could help in an emergency to bring damaged aircraft safely home. All the various electrical installations were tested including bomb circuits, intercommunication (intercom) for the crew to speak from one post to another inside the aircraft.They were thoroughly tried out by the electrician and signal lamps, batteries and circuit fuses were all rigorously tested.

The instrument repairer examined all the flying and navigational equipment and made sure it was in working order. This was no small task in the general scheme of aircraft maintenance. There were engine speed indicators, directional gyros, rate of climb indicators, instruments showing angle of bank, compasses and air speed indicator, and others showing engine temperature and pressure gauges. Petrol bowser drivers also made sure that each aircraft had enough fuel to complete the operation safely.

No.50 Squadron armourers fitting fuses and bomb tail units

Last, but certainly not least, the armourer tested the hydraulically operated gun turrets, cleaned all the machine guns, and saw that all bomb releases in the bomb bay were in full working order.

It was also the Squadron armourers responsibility to provide the right bomb load to each aircraft and check that the bombs were properly housed and correctly fused, and that all safety devices were in position.

Un-fused bombs litter the dispersal of VN-P "Peter" due to target and bomb load changes at the last moment after D-Day 6th June 1944

When all these details had been attended to the respective tradesmen signed the maintenance Form 700 which stated that all equipment had been tested. This form was taken to the Flight Sergeant, who satisfied himself that all was correct before he too signed the certificate which immediately placed the aircraft as 'Ready for flight'.

Operations Staff:
During the day the Intelligence Officer gathered together all the information on file about the target for that night. Target information had been painstakingly collected over a long period in readiness for such an operation.

At the briefing he would highlight enemy ground and night fighter defences and distinctive landmarks which would help pilots and navigators check their position en-route and over the target. To supplement all this information the I.O. contacted the Group Intelligence Officer to see if he had any fresh information about the target and enemy defences.

The Met Officer awaited a report from the latest Met Flight over enemy territory before putting together his weather forecast covering take-off, en-route, target area and return to base.

The bulk of the work in preparing the aircraft was carried out by the ground staff, but the aircrew nevertheless kept a sharp eye on the various tasks to see that nothing was left undone.

If necessary an air test was carried out by the aircrew in order to check out the engines and various electrical and mechanical systems. The air gunners would also test their guns by firing hundreds of rounds at flame floats dropped into the sea. These flights were also part of the endless training an operational crew undertook to improve their chances of survival.

Because of operational losses and tour expired crews, the Squadron was made up of aircrews with varying degrees of operational experience. The successful aircrews, the Gen men of the Squadron, were the ones who had flown together many thousands of miles and had achieved a high level of understanding and trust in each others ability. This team spirit plus a lot of luck was essential if they were to survive a thirty operation tour.

No.50 Squadron aircraft ready to go to war

The Main Briefing:

The Squadron Commander would read out the Operational Order he had received from Group headquarters and then uncover a large wall map of western Europe showing the routes to be followed. This was neatly indicated by a long piece of coloured tape pinned across the map showing base to target and return routes.

These routes had been carefully chosen in order to avoid flying over known heavily defended areas. A separate board listed the names of the pilots against the call sign of each aircraft taking part in the raid. The take off times for each aircraft and details of the kind of bombs loaded on the aircraft were also displayed. After his general overview of the operation, the Squadron Commander would also pass on any special instructions that he had received from Group Headquarters

The Intelligence Officer then went over the route with the pilots, navigators and bomb aimers pointing out landmarks and drawing special attention to prominent features by which landfall could be recognised. Strong points in the enemy ground defences were indicated and the type of target indicators and route markers that would be used by the Pathfinder squadrons. Questions were answered, and any doubtful elements of his presentation were explained. He was followed by the Met Officer whose weather charts showed the weather conditions in the target area, the type of cloud that could be encountered en-route and the possibility of any ice or fog upon return to base in the early hours of the morning. The Flying Control Officer then briefed the crews about the runway in use for the operation and take off procedures to be followed.

Next, the Wing Commander gave advice on the operation. He had probably been over that part of enemy territory many times before. His words, based on his personal experience, were especially helpful to the sprog crews. The station Group Captain added a few words of encouragement, stressed the importance of the operation, wished the crews good luck, and the briefing was over.

The crews would still have a couple of hours before take off. Some would go to their billets to try and relax while others would go to the mess for their pre-ops meal of bacon and eggs just in case they didn't get back in the morning. Meanwhile the aircraft captains and navigators still had to work out their course within the bomber stream based upon take off times and target estimated time of arrival (ETA).

Next the crews would meet in the locker room and change into their flying kit. Having collected parachutes and safety equipment they would then board the lorries and buses lined up to take them out to their aircraft dispersal.

Final engine run up before leaving the dispersal

Setting the Skellingthorpe Morse code Beacon

The time had arrived for the heavy laden aircraft to be made ready for take-off. An electrical starter trolley was wheeled out; emergency rations were stowed near the collapsible dinghy in case the aircraft had to be abandoned over water.

Meanwhile the armourer gave a final check to bomb load and machine guns.

The crews arrived at their aircraft dispersal and made final checks around the kite, after which they carried out their individual rituals, a last minute cigarette or wetting the rear wheel for good luck. They boarded the aircraft and settled down in their crew take-off positions. Even then there could be a last minute scrub of the operation due to bad weather en-route or in the target area.

A Verey pistol would be fired from the control tower signifying engine start up time had arrived for the waiting bomber crews. With bomb doors closed and engines started each pilot tested his aircraft's controls, ran the engines and assured himself that everything was in order before leaving the dispersal.

Chocks were waved away and at the appointed time the pilot taxied the aircraft to the perimeter track and joined other aircraft weaving their way to the holding point at the end of the runway.

Waiting for the green light to take off and climb away through low cloud

The runway controller gives the green light

After receiving a Green on the Aldis lamp from the controllers caravan, the pilot turned his aircraft onto the end of the main runway and applied the brakes. He then revved the engines, released the brakes and the aircraft slowly moved forward before gaining speed and bouncing slightly on the undercarriage hydraulics under the weight of a full bomb and fuel load.

This was the most critical time as the pilot concentrated to control the aircraft's tendency to swing to port due to the massive torque created by four Merlin engines at full power. The loss of power from one of the engines or a burst tyre could spell instant disaster for the crew. Eventually with most of the runway consumed it struggled free of terra firma. Then, with its undercarriage retracted the Lancaster quickly gained height and disappeared into the fading light.

No.50 Squadron Lancaster ED856 VN-K "King" takes-off at the start of another operation. This veteran of the Battle of Hamburg and Berlin was safely abandoned by the crew over Le Mans in France after suffering severe night fighter damage while returning from Darmstadt 25/26th August 1944

Under low rain clouds a 50 Squadron aircraft turns east to join the Bomber Stream

The Bomber Stream forms over the North Sea and heads for the enemy coast

Pathfinder aircraft lead the way and drop Target Indicators through heavy flack

The crew of VN-B is de-briefed after returning from Stuttgart 1943

Start of Another Day

When each aircraft returned to it's dispersal the ground crew would be waiting. Each aircraft had a faults book in which the Captain noted any mechanical or electrical equipment faults that arose during the flight and had to be rectified before the next operation.

Senior NCOs in charge of each technical trade also inspected the aircraft and recorded petrol, oil and coolant consumption so that the performance of the engines could be assessed.

Also there were times when urgent repairs had to be made when an aircraft returned with serious damage to the airframe and control services after being hit by flak or during a night fighter attack.

Many aircraft returned with one or more engines out of action which highlights the young bomber pilots flying skill and determination to return his aircraft and crew safely to base.

Once all the data had been collected, it was quickly assessed and a decision taken on whether the aircraft was repairable on the Flight line or had to go into the No. 58 Maintenance T2 hangar on the technical site for major repairs.

No. 61 SQUADRON

Thundering Through The Clear Air

Commanding Officers	Date
S/Ldr C H Brill	03/37
W/Cdr C M De Crespigny	09/39
W/Cdr F M Denny	02/40
W/Cdr G H Sheen	05/40
W/Cdr G E Valentine	11/40
W/Cdr C T Weir	09/41
W/Cdr C M Coad	06/42
W/Cdr W M Penman	02/43
W/Cdr R N Stidolph	10/43
W/Cdr A W Doubleday	04/44
W/Cdr W D Pexton	09/44
W/Cdr C W Scott	02/45

On the 16th November 1943 No. 50 Squadron were joined at Skellingthorpe by No.61 (The Lincoln Imp) Squadron headed by Wing Commander Reginald Stidolph. Both squadrons were expanding during this time and heavily engaged in the 'Battle of Berlin'. This six month campaign during the winter months of 1943/44 cost Bomber Command 1,100 heavy bomber aircraft and the loss of over 8,000 highly trained air crew. The equivalent of 60 front line squadrons.

Air crew of Bomber Command led a very surreal existence during the Second World War. Over a very short periods of time they had to quickly adjust mentally from mundane duties around the airfield, or going for a night out with the boys, to flying stressful dangerous bombing operations over hostile enemy territory.

As a result many suffered from anxiety and some found it impossible to complete their tour of 30 operations and were branded LMF (Lack of Moral Fibre) and posted away with loss of rank to carry out non-flying duties.

S/L Sid Beard   W/Cdr Reg Stidolph   S/L John Woodruffe

The above photograph was taken at RAF Skellingthorpe on the 2nd January 1944 and shows No. 61 Squadron's Commanding Officer, Wing Commander R N Stidolph and his two Flight Commanders.

TARGET FOR TONIGHT

On the 5/6th of January 1944 No.61 Squadron took part in a night raid against industrial targets and port installations in the German Baltic town of Stettin.

Wing Commander Stidolph put himself and crew on the Squadron Battle Order for that night and was allocated Lancaster JB138 QR-J "Just Jane" for the operation.

They took off at 00:02hrs and headed east out over the North Sea to join a bomber stream consisting of 347 Lancasters and 10 Halifaxes. At the same time 13 Mosquito aircraft set out on a diversionary Berlin raid to draw German night fighters away from the main force target area.

After flying north for two hours the raiders turned east over the Danish coast near the island of Sylt and after reaching the Baltic sea they hugged the north German coast until the target was identified by the leading Pathfinder aircraft. These aircraft marked the aiming point in the centre of Stettin at 03:30hrs with red and green Target Indicators. Accurate bombing by the main force resulted in the central and western districts of the town suffering heavily from fire and blast damage. Eight ships were also sunk in the harbour

While the Mosquito Berlin raid had been successful in diverting night fighters from the main force during the attack, the returning bomber crews soon found the German night fighter controllers had realised Stettin was the main objective and vectored the fighters to pursue them.

At 03:58hrs while flying west over the Baltic sea towards Denmark. W/Cdr Stidolph and crew were suddenly traumatized by a terrific noise and felt their aircraft judder with the impact of exploding cannon shells fired by a German night fighter. Neither of the Lancs two gunners saw the twin engine Me 210 attack from the rear port quarter until they saw flashes of light from the enemy aircrafts deadly twin 20mm cannon.

The rear gunner, P/O Pullman quickly instructed the skipper to "corkscrew port" as both gunners returned fire and saw the Messerschmitt climb and curve around for another attack. They continued firing as it climbed and were rewarded by seeing the fighter's starboard engine suddenly burst into flame and trail black smoke. The gunners ceased fire and the mid-upper, Sgt. Gardener reported to the skipper that the night fighter had been hit and had dived away from view.

Disoriented by the corkscrew manoeuvre in the darkness of the cockpit, Stidolph gradually got the aircraft under control and called up the crew over the intercom to report any injuries or damage they could see from their crew positions.The rear gunner reported a large hole in the port tail-fin and Sgt. Barnes-Moss the wireless operator reported cannon shell splinters had penetrated the main fuselage between the mid-upper turret and wireless operator positions causing damage to the R/T, visual Monica and Gee navigation equipment thus making them all u/s .During the initial attack by the night fighter, the Lancs port-outer engine had been hit and set on fire so skipper Stidolph immediately ordered Sgt. Anthony the flight engineer to shut down the engine, extinguish the fire and feather the propeller to reduce drag. Unfortunately this action also disabled the rear turret as it is powered by this engine.

Wing Commander Stidolph then found the aircraft was practically unmanageable on three engines, so he decided to throttle the starboard outer right back and fly on just the two inner engines set on maximum boost and revs. He then ordered navigator F/O Dyer to get an accurate fix on their position and work out a more direct route back to base. Dyer was assisted by bomb aimer F/O Aley who was laying in the nose of the aircraft looking out for any recognisable ground features and heavily defended areas.

In the dark hostile environment, with the aircraft flying just above stalling speed and vibrating with battle damage progress was slow. Four hours later and down to 4000ft the aircraft crossed the Dutch coast on the last leg of their journey home over the dreaded North Sea. At 09:55 after being in the air for nearly 10 hours "Just Jane" landed at RAF Matlaske on the north Norfolk coast with just 9 gallons of petrol left in it's fuel tanksThe crew were exhausted by the night's traumatic experience and after debrief and breakfast they tried to sleep for a few hours before their transport arrived to take them back to Skellingthorpe. However most of them found sleep impossible and in total contrast to the events of the previous night they decided to go into the small town of Cromer by the sea and enjoyed a few peaceful hours relaxation.

They all found it refreshing but in the back of their minds knew it was inevitably that within a few days their names would appeared once again on the Squadron Battle Order for them to go back to war.

During the Battle of Berlin in the winter of 1943/44 air crew of Bomber Command knew they only had a 1 in 3 chance of completing a tour of 30 operations over enemy territory. Even so, many of Wing Commander Stidolph's crew were second tour men who had returned to the Squadron knowing full well the odds of surviving a second tour was against them.

Rear gunner Pilot Officer John Pullman was one of them and received the Distinguished Flying Cross (DFC) for his actions that night.

While skipper Wing Commander Reginald Stidolph was awarded an Immediate DFC for his outstanding leadership, skill and determination in safely bringing home his crew and damaged aircraft.

Sixteen aircraft (4.5%) of the main force failed to return to their bases

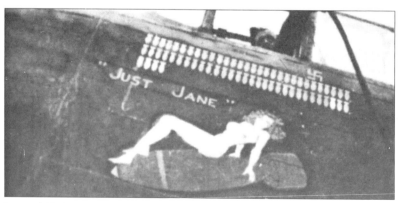

Lancaster JB138 QR-J "Just Jane" was repaired and went on to complete 123 operations before being transferred to a training squadron in February 1945.

AIRCRAFT & CREWS

On the Skellingthorpe domestic front there was a shortage of accommodation so No.61 Squadron transferred to RAF Coningsby for a two month detachment in February 1944, while contractors increased accommodation and facilities on the airfield.

The Squadron returned to Skellingthorpe on 15th of April and joined No. 50 Squadron in attacking pre-invasion communication targets in France and Holland.

After the D-Day landings in Normandy on the 6th June 1944, both Squadrons supported the Allied ground forces with daylight raids against enemy troop concentrations south-east of Paris. In August Bomber Command returned once again to the hostile sky over Germany but also concentrated on V1 and V2 rocket launch and storage sites, railway yards and fuel storage depots in France.

No. 61 Squadron senior officers including W/C Reg Stidolph (4th right) with Flight commanders S/L Sid Beard and S/L John Woodruff and their Navigation, Signals and Bombing Leaders.

Lancaster LL744 VN-B was flown by the Beetham crew - January 1944

F/L Mike Beetham's crew: L-R Fred Ball (RG) Les Bartlett (BA)
Mike Beetham Frank Swinyard (N) Reg Payne (W/Op) Don Moore (F/E) Jock Higgins (MU)

F/L Mike Beetham DFC was only 20 years old when he completed his tour of 30 operations. The crew went to Berlin ten times during the winter of 1943/44 "Battle of Berlin" They lost an engine over Augsburg, got shot up over Leipzig and baled out on a training flight when an engine caught fire.

F/L Beetham stayed in the RAF after the War to become "Marshal of the Royal Air Force".

End of tour photo in April 1944 of Flt/Lt Bernard Fitch DFC & crew in front of their aircraft Lancaster LL777 QR-S "Sugar". The nose art was called "Royal Pontoon".
L-R: Len Whitehead (MU) John Taylor (F/E) John Kershaw (W/Op) Les Cromerty (RG) Bernard Fitch (P) Sid Jennings (N) Alfie Lyons (BA)

Bernard Fitch and crew flew their tour of operations during the hard fought 1943/44 winter "Battle of Berlin". No.61 Squadron lost 22 crews during this period and the Fitch crew became the first crew to complete a tour of operations since August 1943.

During his 28 Ops tour Bernard Fitch had many lucky escapes while flying over enemy territory from both flak and night fighters attack.

On one occasion he was looking ahead out of the aircrafts windscreen when he suddenly saw the dimly lit face of a German night fighter pilot as the enemy aircraft flashed by only 20ft above his cockpit canopy going in the opposite direction. Len Whitehead, the mid-upper gunner was also alarmed by the near miss and watched the night fighter make a quick 180 degree turn and then flew for several minutes just out of range of his guns on the starboard side. Although the well armed twin engine Ju 88 could have attacked and possibly shot down QR-S. The Luftwaffe pilot decided to turn away and hunt down an easier unsuspecting victim.

Lancaster DV397 "QR-W"

This Lancaster was one of 72 aircraft that failed to return from the 24/25th March 1944 night raid on Berlin. The reason for such a high number of aircraft lost on this raid was because the attacking bombers en-countered strong north winds of over 125 mph while flying over the Baltic sea. The Pathfinders had difficulty in marking the target area as the wind carried the Target Indicators to the south-west of the city. Some aircraft arrived over Berlin too early and 14 were shot down by night fighters while others were downed by the city's flak defences.

The scattered bomber stream returned over the north German plain and many aircraft strayed over heavily defended areas and fell victim to radar-predicted flak batteries that ringed the industrial Ruhr valley.

While considerable damage was inflicted on the German capital Bomber Command's heavies were destined never to return to the dreaded Big City.

The "Battle of Berlin" finally ended a week later on the 30/31st March 1944 with the disastrous Nurenberg raid. When ninety-five heavy bombers were shot down over enemy territory and another fifteen damaged aircraft crashed in England.

Lancaster ND876 VN-Z "Zulu" failed to return to Skellingthorpe from Munich on 24/25th April 1944 . Crew: F/O L Durham DFC, Sgt. F P Brown, F/S E S Jones, P/O R G Brock DFC, F/S D L Reynolds, F/S N Jackson and F/S G R Casaubon.

This was F/O Len Durham and crews 30th and final sortie of their tour.

VN-Z "Zulu "was part of a main force of 234 Lancasters for this night raid on the city of Munich. While on their bombing run over the target the aircraft took a direct hit from flak breaking it into two sections. There were no survivors. However the intense flak and searchlights defences did not prevent the low flying Marker Force of 16 Mosquitoes laying down their target indicators very accurately on the aiming point.

The following Bomber Stream aircraft released their bombs on the centre of the city causing major damage to domestic and public buildings. They were also successful in damaging railway installations and industrial sites

While less than 100 people died in the raid, over 30,000 were left homeless. Nine Lancasters (3.5%) were lost from the main force.

No.50 Squadron Lancaster LM429 VN-T "Tommy" returns to Skellingthorpe on a rainy February morning in 1944. Three months later on the 11/12th May 1944 "Tommy" was shot down with 11 other 5 Group Lancasters while taking part in a very successful attack on the Lille railway yards.

Luck be a Lady tonight

F/O A.E. Stone DFC

Lancaster ED860 QR-N "Nan"

Nineteen year old Arthur Edward (Ted) Stone from Somerset volunteered to join the RAF in July1941 and was accepted for aircrew. He was mobilised in late October and after Initial Training at Blackpool he was posted to No.11 Elementary Flying Training School at RAF Shawbury where he attained the required grade on Tiger Moth aircraft.

In June 1942 Sgt. Ted Stone was shipped to Canada and then on to an Advanced Flying Training School in Georgia U.S.A. Where, after single and multi-engine aircraft training was awarded his "Wings".

He was then posted back to England in January1943 for navigation and formation training in twin engine Airspeed Oxfords.

In June 1943 he progressed to the Operational Training Unit (O.T.U.) at RAF Cottesmore and formed a five man crew consisting of himself, F/S J F Mills (Navigator) Sgt. W J Sinclair (Bomb Aimer) Sgt. T Francis (Wireless Operator) and Sgt. A Kane (Rear Gunner) . Where they trained as a crew in twin engine war weary Wellington bombers.

After successfully completing this operational training course in early October 1943 Ted Stone accepted a commission and promoted to Pilot Officer.

The crew then moved on to No.1654 Heavy Conversion Unit (H.C.U.) at RAF Wigsley. There he selected a Flight Engineer, Sgt. A Dick and a Mid- Upper gunner Sgt. G E Cunningham to complete his seven man heavy bomber crew.

Over the next three months they flew many hours in the four engine Lancaster heavy bomber thus gaining valuable experience on how to survive a tour of ops by carrying out various aircraft emergency procedures, navigation and bombing exercises on long cross country flights at night over the U.K..

By the end of December 1943, P/O Ted Stone had logged 193 daylight and 94 night flying hours on multi-engine aircraft. His instructors at Wigsley considered him to be an average pilot and ready to join a front line squadron in Bomber Command.

During the winter months of 1943/44, air crew had only a one in three chance of surviving a tour of 30 operations over enemy territory. This was the situation P/O Ted Stone and crew faced when they reported for duty with No.61 Squadron of No.5 Group at RAF Skellingthorpe on the 5th January 1944 as a replacement crew.

The Battle of Berlin was at it's height and Ted's name was soon on the Squadron Battle Order. He was to fly as second pilot with S/L E H Moss DFC on a night bombing raid against Brunswick in order to gain operational experience.

After such initiation sorties the Squadron Wing Commander usually tried to give new crews a, so called, easy target at the start of their tour. However for P/O Ted Stone and crew their first operation together was on the 20th January 1944. The target was Berlin, the dreaded "Big City".

During their 7 hour 45 minute sortie in Lancaster W4315 QR-Q "Queenie", they managed to avoid German night fighters and bombed the target area from 25,000ft.

They returned to Berlin again on the 27th/28th January and this time flew in Lancaster ED860 QR-N "Nan" on it's 62nd operation.
The skipper of QR-N's regular crew was Flt/Lt H N Scott, who flew the aircraft twenty-one times during his tour, including eleven times to Berlin.

The Scott crew finished their tour of operations at the end of February1944 so Ted Stone asked his Flight Commander, S/L John Woodruffe if he could take over Lancaster ED860 QR-N as his regular aircraft.

Woodruffe agreed and over the next four months P/O Stone and crew flew another 21 operational sorties in her. The last one being on the 21st/22an May 1944 with a raid on Duisburg. This was QR-N's 92nd operational sortie.
During their tour, the Stone crew flew18 bombing sorties against heavily defended targets in Germany and another 11 in occupied France.

On the 31st May 1944, Wing Commander Arthur Doubleday made the crew none operational, tour completed.

P/O Ted Stone and crew had survived a tour of operations s during a period of very heavy losses by Bomber Command's front line squadrons. In order to survive you had to have a good crew and a big slice of luck.

After the crew completed their tour they agreed that the first baby girl born to any of them would be named after their "Lucky Lady QR-N "Nan" who brought them safely home on 22 occasions. As it turned out Ted's daughter was the first to born at the end of 1944 and was promptly named Jennifer Nan Stone.

In August 1944 Ted Stone was promoted to Flying Officer and awarded the Distinguished Flying Cross (DFC).

Citation:
"For completing many successful operations against the enemy, in which he displayed high skill, fortitude and devotion to duty"

28th of June 1944 : Corporal Ellis Ainley oversees the painting of the 100th bomb symbol on Lancaster ED860 QR-N "Nan" watched by a proud ground crew.

Lancaster ED860 entered RAF Bomber Command service on the 14th April 1943 with No.156 Pathfinder Squadron at RAF Warboys in Cambridgeshire.

After completing 25 sorties it was transferred to No.61 Squadron at RAF Skellingthorpe on the 20th August 1943.

Over the next six months it was the only Lancaster to fly on all 20 Berlin sorties during the "Battle of Berlin".

It completed a total of 105 Bombing sorties with 61 Squadron before it crashed on take-off on the 28th October 1944.

QR-N "Nan" beat No.50 Squadron VN-G "George by 7 days to become the first Lancaster in Bomber Command to complete 100 operations over enemy territory
.

With a hundred bomb symbols displayed the aircraft is photographed with F/O Basil Turner (centre) and crew in addition to the proud ground staff who were responsible for keeping the aircraft flying.

F/O Turner's crew was multi-national and consisted of :
Sgt. R Brown RAF (FE) W/O G.W. James RCAF (N) F/O E. Jones RAAF (BA)
Sgt. H. Edwards RAF (W/Op) Sgt. G.W. McDonell RCAF (MU) and Sgt. N.W. Pettin RCAF (RG)

This crew flew 14 operations in QR-N between the 27th May to the 5th August 1944.

At the end of his tour Basil Turner was awarded the Distinguished Flying Cross (DFC)

QR-N "Nan" is bombed up before F/O Norman Hoad and crew set off to attack U-Boat pens in Bordeaux 11th August 1944

This crew : F/O N.E. Hoad (P) Sgt. C.S. Webb (FE) F/O K..W. Ball (N) F/O W.H. Pullen (BA) Sgt. C.P. Boyd (W/Op) Sgt. N. England (MU) and Sgt. C.B. Embury (RG) flew in QR-N on six occasions. The last being on 29/30th August on a deep penetration flight to Konigsburg and suffered severe damaged from a night fighters attack over the target.

The Hoad crew continued their tour of operations in Lancaster ME595 QR-R.

However their luck ran out on 14/15th October 1944 over Brunswick when they were attacked by night fighters and shot down.

F/O Norman Hoad and four other members of his crew managed to escape by parachute and became POWs

After the war Norman Hoad stayed in the RAF and was promoted over the next twenty years to the rank of Air Vice Marshall CVO, CBE,AFC

Pilots route map

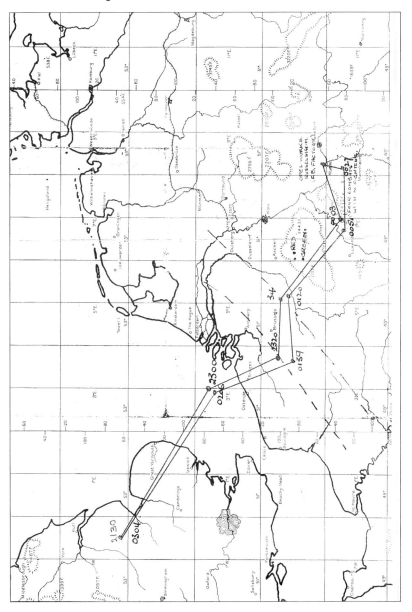

The skipper of QR-N on the 12th /13th of August 1944 was F/O Norman Hoad

His map shows the route to Russelsheim where they bombed the Opel works. Also where the aircraft was attacked four time by a night fighter

The pride of No.50 Squadron Lancaster ED588 VN-G "George" displays 90 bomb symbols in May 1944. In the background is QR-L of No. 61 Squadron

On 19th of June 1944 Flying Officer Howell Enoch became the aircrafts regular skipper completing 23 sorties of his tour. This included the aircraft's 100th sortie on the 4/5th July 1944 when the crew bombed the V1 workshops and storage facility in the caves of St. Leu D'Esserent

F/O Enoch and crew add another completed operation to VN-G after returning from bombing railway yards at Courtrai on the 20/21st July 1944.

The last time the crew flew in VN-G was to Konigsburg on the 26/27 August before going on leave. They were a lucky crew as the aircraft failed to return from it's next operation to the same target on the 29/30 August 1944

No.50 Sqdn VN-G "George" & No.61 Sqdn QR-N "Nan" taxi out for another daylight raid in August 1944.

On the 29th/30th August 1944 both aircraft flew on a deep penetration raid to Konigsberg and met heavy night fighter opposition.

VN-G "George" was shot down and crashed in Sweden. Skipper F/O Tony Carver and five other members of his crew were killed and are buried in Sweden.

Only W/Op Sgt. E. Match survived.

While QR-N "Nan" with F/O Hoad at the controls managed to get home after suffering damage from a night fighter. Upon inspection the ground staff discovered a live 20mm cannon shell lodged in the starboard wing route.

In addition Hoad had to fly the aircraft manually for 10 hours 45 minutes because "George " the Auto Pilot became U/S on the way to the target.

The aircraft went into the hangar for repairs and didn't return to operational duty again until the 23rd October 1944 when a new replacement crew notched up it's 130th operation against Flak batteries near Flushing.

On the 28th October QR-N was again allocated to the sprog crew for a night attack on the German U-Boat pens at Bergen in Norway. Unfortunately the nineteen year old Australian pilot F/O Laurence Pearse had never taken off with a fully laden Lancaster at night before and wasn't used to the slow acceleration of a fully loaded Lancaster.

As a result he applied full power too early before he had full rudder control and the aircraft swung off the runway hitting a glim lamp which burst a tyre and the undercarriage collapsed.

The resulting ground loop tore off the starboard outer engine and part of the wing spilling high octane fuel from ruptured tanks. By the time the aircraft finally came to a halt the heavy fuel and bomb load on board had crushed the bomb bay doors and lower fuselage.

Wireless Operator Bill Perry wrote the following account of the crash in his War Diary:

Saturday 28th October 1944
"**Ops on Bergen in "N" Nan (night). Did not take-off as plane swung on take-off and crashed at 65 miles per hour with full bomb load on board. Undercart collapsed and starboard outer engine torn off . Bomb bay wrecked and nose smashed in. Nan is a complete write off.**

We were very lucky the bombs didn't go off. Jock Murray the engineer suffered the only injury when he cut his face while abandoning the aircraft.

"SHE WAS A LUCKY KITE RIGHT TO THE END"

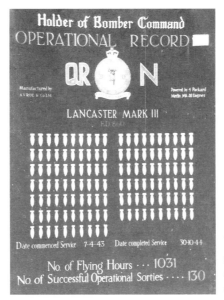

This panel was displayed in No. 61 Squadron Officers Mess

RAF Skellingthorpe

F/O Laurence Pearse and crew pose in front of their replacement aircraft QR-X. L-R R Pettigrew (N) J Murray (FE) R Gillander (RG) L Pearse (P) D Baker (B/A)R Barker (MU) Bill Perry (W/Op)

No.61 Squadron Navigators

This is the Operations Log of Air Gunner Sgt. Ken Johnson who was a member of F/O Harry Watkins crew. The following gives an indication of the number of operations No.61 Squadron flew in the three months following the Normandy landings on D-DAY the 6th June 1944.

Ops No	Date	Lancaster Serial No	Destination	Target
June 1944				
1	19	ND896	Watten	V1 storage in woodland
2	21/22	ND867	Gelsenkirchen	Synthetic oil plants
3	23/24	ND867	Limoges	Railway Yards
4	24	ND867	Prouville	V1 sites
5	27/28	ND867	Vitry	Railway yards
6	29	R5856	Beauvoir	V1 sites
July 1944				
7	04/05	R5856	St Leu D'Esserent	V1 Storage mushroom caves
8	07/08	LM590	St Leu D'Esserent	V1 Storage mushroom caves
9	23/24	LM590	Kiel	Industry & Naval installations
10	24/25	LM590	Donges	Oil refinery & storage
11	25	LM590	St Cyr	Airfield & signals depot
12	26/27	ND896	Givors (Lyon)	Railway Yards
13	28/29	ND896	Stuttgart	Industry
14	30	LL911	Caumont	Normandy Army support
15	31	LL911	Joigny La Roche	Railway Yards
August 1944				
16	01	LL911	Mont Candon	V1 Sites
17	02	LL911	Bois de Cassan	V1 storage sites
21	09/10	LL911	Foret de Chattellerault	Oil storage dumps
22	12/13	LL911	Russelheim	Opel motor plant

23	13	LL911	Bordeaux	Oil storage
24	15	LL911	Gilze-Rijen	Night fighter base in Holland
25	16/17	LL911	Stettin	Port installation & industry
26	19	LL911	La Pallice	Oil storage
27	31	LL911	Rollencourt	V2 storage sites (N France)

September 1944

28	05	LL911	Brest	Gun positions outside Brest
29	10	LL911	Le Havre	Normandy Army support
30	11/12	LL911	Darmstadt	Industry
31	17	ME732	Boulogne	Army support
32	23/24	LL911	Dortmund-Ems canal	Transport
33	26/27	LL911	Karlsruhe	Industry

The Watkins crew - August 1944 L-R Doug Hockin (N) Harry Watkins (P) Fred Jowitt (E) Ken Johnson (MU) Johnny Ware (W/Op) Hugh Green (RG) Edgar Ray (BA)

After completing his tour of 33 ops with No. 61 Squadron, Ken and his skipper volunteered to join No.9 Squadron at RAF Bardney and flew another nine operations by the end of hostilities.

Lancaster EE176 "QR-M" Mickey The Moocher flew 128 Ops before being retired in November 1944 to an Operational Training Unit (OTU)

Lancaster LL842 VN-F "Fox" failed to return from Stuttgart 24/25th July 1944.

The aircraft was named after the London West End star Phyllis Dixey, the forces favourite Striptease artist.

Ground crew prepare Lancaster PB759 "QR-N" for another raid. The aircraft was lost with F/O B.S. Tasker and crew on the 8/9th February 1945 Politz raid.

The Politz operation was carried out by 475 Lancasters and 10 Mosquitos.

It was planned to attack the target in two waves. The first wave consisted only of aircraft belonging to No.5 Group. Twin engine Mosquitos of their Pathfinder Force marked the target at low level for the following bomber squadrons.

Pathfinders of No.8 Group then followed up and marked the target for the second wave of Lancasters of No.1 Group.

In clear weather conditions the bombing of both waves was extremely accurate and severe damage was done to the important Synthetic Oil plant. Thereby stopping oil production until after the war.

Albert Speer the head of German war material production described this raid as a big setback to Germany's war effort. Bomber Command lost 12 Lancasters (2.5%)

REAR GUNNER'S STORY

James Flowers aged 18 in 1944   *2008 Squadron reunion*

Henry (Taffy) Flowers and I joined the RAF on the 6th of March 1944 at the Aircrew Induction Centre, Lords Cricket Ground, London. When the name H.J. Flowers was called out we both stepped forward. Little did we know then we would become friends and fly together in the same bomber crew. After kitting out we moved to St John's Wood for medicals and inoculations.

With the Germans having renewed their blitz on London, we spent many nights squatting on the stairs listening to bombs explode. Two weeks later while on the train to RAF Bridgenorth for basic training. I looked out of the train window and saw the extent of the bomb damage to greater London since 1940 and vowed to return the compliment.

From Bridgenorth we moved to RAF Stormey Down, South Wales for Air Gunner Training. On successfully completing this course we were presented with our A/G brevet and promoted to Sergeant.

Next we moved to the Operational Training Unit (OTU) at Husbands Bosworth where Henry and I became members of New Zealand pilot John Strathern Lawrey's bomber crew.

Our next posting was to the Heavy Conversion Unit (HCU) at RAF Wigsley and then to RAF Syerston to the Lancaster Finishing School. (LFS)

In January 1945 after many UK cross country flights in the four engine Lancaster we at last finished our training and posted to RAF Skellingthorpe for active duty with No.50 Squadron of No.5 Group, Bomber Command.

Just before take off for a raid on Bohlem, Germany on 4th March 1945.
L to R. H.W.Kent WOP. Henry. J. Flowers (Taffy) MUG. Frank Wallis BA. Arthur Smth FE.
H.James Flowers RG. John S.Lawrey Pilot.

Two hours or so into the Bohlem trip there was a blinding flash just behind us as two bombers collided and then exploded in mid-air leaving a trail of burning wreckage. Those unseen aircraft in the bomber Stream now seemed very menacing. That thought really focused my mind !!

Sometime later I saw an Me 109 night fighter emerge from the 10-10th cloud some two thousand feet below. Gradually it moved from our starboard beam to dead astern at the same height and came within firing range.

I fired and saw the tracer bullets from my four machine guns rip into the German night fighter and it immediately dived straight down into the clouds.

As we reached the target area another Me 109 attacked us. I quickly aimed and fired but as I did so the back of my illuminated gun sight fell out. The bright light temporarily blinding me and as I frantically struggled to put the gun sight together again I fully expecting bullets to come pinging into my turret at any moment. As my night vision gradually returned I was amazed and relieved to find that the Me 109 had disappeared.
.

During a 10 hour night trip to bomb the synthetic oil plant at Lutzkendorf on 14/15th March 1945, we came under attack again. Just after leaving the target area a fighter flare burst above us brightly lighting up the night sky. Within seconds an FW 190 attacked us from the starboard beam. I opened fire and alerted the skipper who threw the Lancaster into a wild Corkscrew manoeuvre. Moments later I saw a faint movement down on the port side and saw a Ju 88 trying to get underneath us in order to fire it's upward firing twin cannon. So I quickly swung my turret round and engaged it with a hail of .303 ammunition. Both fighters eventually broke away but they returned many times in an attempt to destroy us

Our navigator recorded the night fighter attacks lasted 26 minutes before we lost them. During this time I used all 10,000 rounds supplied to the rear turret. To this day I still ask myself the question "How did we get away with it"?

Whilst a member of John Lowrey's crew flying operations with Bomber Command. We survived attacks from Me109 and FW190 single engine fighters. Twin engine Ju88s and Me262 jet fighters. Almost blasted out of the sky with heavy flak and dropping like a stone from 11,000ft to 500ft plus numerous near misses with other aircraft while flying blind at night.

ALL VERY EXCITING BUT NOTHING SPECIAL, JUST THE NORMAL SORT OF THINGS WHICH HAPPENED TO MOST BOMBER CREWS DURING THE SECOND WORLD WAR

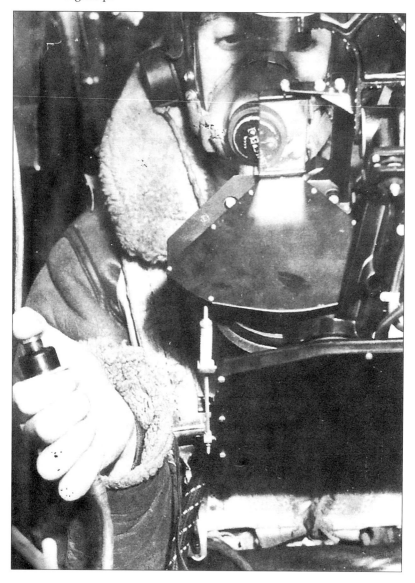

Bomb Aimer looks through his bomb site ready to press the release button

*RAF Skellingthorpe station commander Group Captain Jefferson presents
the "CAMROSE BOMBING TROPHY" to No. 50 Squadron Bomb Aimers.
In the centre is Sgt. Ernie Manning and to his left Sgt. Ernie Brown.
This No. 5 Group Trophy was awarded for accurate bombing.*

No. 50 SQUADRON 1945

Operational Performance 1939 - 45

Aircraft	Raids`	Sorties	Losses
Hampden	368	2,299	57 (2.5%)
Manchester	34	126	7 (5.6%)
Lancaster	365	4,710	112 (2.4)
Total	**767**	**7,135**	**176 (2.5%)**

Summary:
No.50 Squadron flew most sorties in No.5 Group and the third highest in Bomber Command

No. 61 SQUADRON 1945

Operational Performance 1939 - 45

Aircraft	Raids	Sorties	Losses
Hampden	283	1,339	28 (2%)
Manchester	44	197	12 (6%)
Lancaster	377	4,546	116 (2.5%)
Total	704	6,082	156 (2.6%)

Summary:
No. 61 Squadron carried out more raids using the Avro Lancaster than any other squadron and flew the second highest total number of raids in Bomber Command

THE WAR IN EUROPE IS OVER

Jubilant 61 Squadron air crew run to the Mess to start celebrating

VE Day 8th May 1945

There was no stand down at RAF Skellingthorpe as some aircraft from both squadrons took-off for airfields on the continent of Europe to carry out Operation Exodus.

Their mission was to bring back to England some of the 75,000 prisoners of war. The crews who were flying to German and French airfields listened to the BBC on the aircrafts radio sets to the momentous announcements of the German surrender.

Later in the month after Operation Exodus had been completed. Both squadrons set about clearing the airfield dispersals of un-fused 500lb bombs by loading them on the aircraft and dropping them in designated zones in the English Channel.

W/O Ivor Soar flying QR-Y over France during Operation Exodus - May 1945

Meanwhile skipper P/O Reg Deer and Nav. Fred Reeves wait for take-off

Throughout V E day at Skellingthorpe preparations were in full swing to clear and decorate one of the hangars for an "All Ranks" party and dance.

RAF buses and lorries were sent out to Lincoln and local villages to bring in the girls to share the celebrations.

RAF airfields throughout Bomber Command celebrated Victory in Europe

After five years of war and an uncertain future it was a day of very mixed emotions for everyone associated with both squadrons.

F/Lt R H Hamer summarised the historic events of May 1945 and wrote down his personal feelings in the No.61 Squadron Operations Record Book

"May 1945 was a month of joys and disappointments. The first being the news of victory in Europe and the second the breaking up of the old squadrons"

CITY OF LINCOLN

VE Celebrations

4TH JUNE, 1945

2.45 p.m.   Parade of Navy, Army, R.A.F. and other units, from Broadgate, via Melville Street, Pelham Street, St. Mary's Street, High Street, Guildhall Street, Newland, Carholme Road to West Common (Salute at Carholme Road).

2 p.m.   West Common—Horse Show and Gymkhana.

2.30 p.m.   ,,   ,,   —Children's Sports.

4 p.m.   ,,   ,,   —(3/- Ring)—Display by Infantry Training Centre P.T. Team.

4.30 p.m.   ,,   ,,   —Display by N.F.S. (Rear of Grandstand).

3 p.m. to 5 p.m.   ,,   ,,   —Band Concert.

     ,,   ,,   —Children's Swings, Punch and Judy, Sideshows, and Donkeys.

N.B.—Owing to restrictions imposed by the Divisional Food Officer there will be NO food, tea or other similar drinks at the West Common. Please bring your own.

3.30 p.m. to 5 p.m.   Arboretum—Band Concert.

3.30 p.m. to 5 p.m.   Boultham Park—Band Concert.

7 p.m. to 10 p.m.   Arboretum—Open-Air Dancing.

7 p.m. to 10 p.m.   Boultham Park—Open-Air Dancing.

                  J. H. SMITH, Town Clerk.

TOWN CLERK'S OFFICE.
CORPORATION OFFICES, LINCOLN.
30th MAY. 1945   E.10

The Official Programme of Events:

Celebrations at the Stone Bow in Lincoln

RAF Waddington's Group Captain leads the parade followed by the Wing Commanders from RAF Waddington, RAF Skellingthorpe and RAF Bardney.

Women's Auxiliary Air Force

RAF personnel from RAF Waddington, RAF Skellingthorpe and RAF Bardney

Flypast of No. 50 Squadron Lancasters (R/T code name "Pilgrim") and No. 61 Squadron Lancasters (R/T code name "Spotnose")

With V. E. celebrations over a member of the Womens Auxiliary Air Force (WAAF) makes her way to Lincoln Central railway station to go home on leave.

Lancaster QR-Y lifts off from RAF Skellingthorpe's main runway

POST WAR YEARS

In the Autumn of 1945 the airfield became none operational and placed under Care and Maintenance. All the bomb stock and other dangerous equipment was taken away for disposal and the hangars were used by No.58 Maintenance Unit for storage.

Later the Control tower was used by Flying Training Command when the main runway was used as a Relief Landing Ground for aircraft based at RAF Swinderby.

RAF Skellingthorpe was officially closed in 1952 and it's buildings dismantled over the next few years.

The old Control Tower / Watch Office (1960)

Emergency landing strip for this Vampire trainer from RAF Swinderby in 1955

For many years after the war the airfield hutted accommodation was used by ex-serviceman families until they could be re-housed

Boundary changes brought the site into the City of Lincoln and the new Birchwood housing estate began to encroach across the airfield

Birchwood Residential Estate

Today very little remains of the old airfield for the veterans who make a pilgrimage to the No.50 & 61 Squadron Memorial on Birchwood Avenue.

Here they remember their old comrades in blue, whose youthful optimism made bearable all the tragic events and hardships they endured while serving at RAF Skellingthorpe over sixty-five years ago.

During the war years I lived only two miles away from the airfield and even now remember the almost nightly tumult of sound generated by 30 Lancaster aircraft as they took-off on their nocturnal bombing operations. Then I would be woken by the sound of returning aircraft racing across the early morning sky to be first home to this primit airfield code named **"BLACK SWAN".**

IN REMEMBRANCE

Sadly the victory over tyranny could not be achieved without loss of life.

Between September 1939 and May 1945 Bomber Command sustained a total of 55,563 fatalities while training or on flying operations against Germany.

Of these No.50 Squadron suffered 1,002 aircrew and ground staff fatalities and No.61 Squadron 981

During the time these squadrons flew operations from RAF Skellingthorpe they lost approximately 1,250 air crew when 208 aircraft failed to return.

Two memorials are dedicated in remembrance of the young men and women who lost their lives while serving with these two bomber squadrons.

Set in a memorial garden by the villagers of Skellingthorpe. The plaque has a poignant epitaph engraved upon it

This memorial was erected on the Birchwood housing estate by No.50 & No.61 Squadron Association close to the site of the only remaining section of perimeter track of RAF Skellingthorpe

Inside the Birchwood Estate Community Centre there is a museum dedicated to N° 50 & N°61 Squadron. While behind the building can be seen this strip of perimeter track that led to N° 50 Squadron aircraft dispersals.

1944

2010

ACKNOWLEDGEMENTS

I would like to thank the veterans of No. 50 and No.61 Squadron for their personal wartime stories and photographs. Also the following organisations for their generous help in connection with the preparation of this book. Without their help this book could not have been written.

No. 50 & No.61 Squadron Association

The Public Records Office at Kew

The Imperial War Museum, London

The Royal Air Force Museum at Hendon

Bomber Command Association

The Lincolnshire Echo

Also a special thanks to Reg Payne ex- Wireless Operator with No.50 Squadron 1943/44, for allowing me to use his excellent paintings for the book cover

Derek Brammer

RAF Skellingthorpe

RAF Skellingthorpe